This book belongs to:

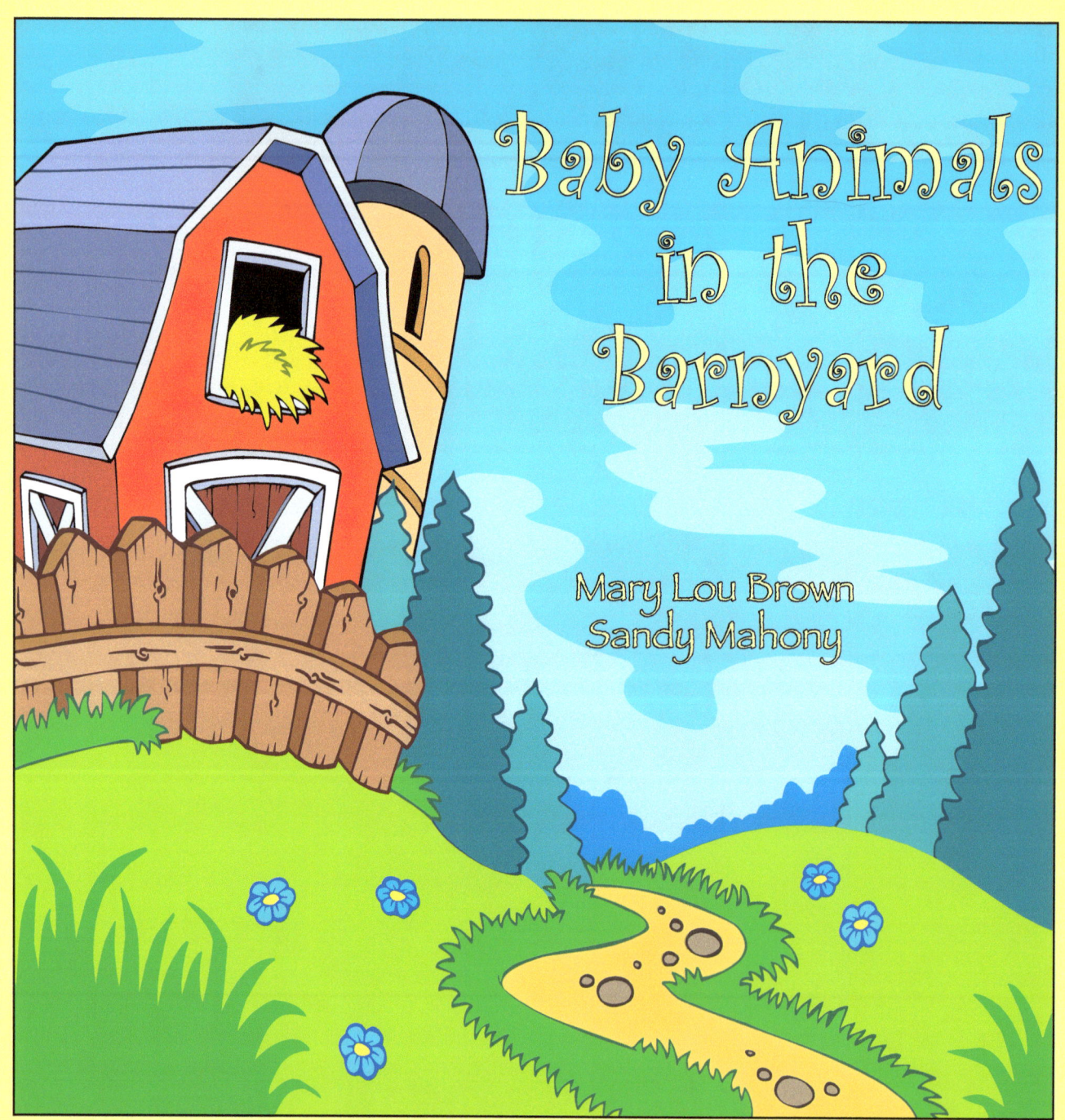

Baby Animals in the Barnyard

Mary Lou Brown
Sandy Mahony

Library of Congress Control Number: 2016904097
CreateSpace Independent Publishing Platform
North Charleston, SC

Lamb, lamb, how are you today?

Baa, baa, baa, come out to play!

Piglet, how are you today?

Oink, oink, oink, come out to play!

Chick, chick, how are you today?

Cheep, cheep, cheep, come out to play!

Colt, colt, how are you today?

Neigh, neigh, neigh, come out to play!

Calf, calf, how are you today?

Moo, moo, moo, come out to play!

Bunny, how are you today?

Squeak, squeak, squeak, come out to play!

Donkey colt, how are you today?

Hee-haw, hee-haw, come out to play!

Hatchlings, how are you today?

Chirp, chirp, chirp, come out to play!

Kitten, how are you today?

Mew, mew, mew, come out to play!

Squirrel pup, how are you today?

Chitter, chatter, come out to play!

Pinkie, how are you today?

Eek, eek, eek, come out to play!

Duckling, how are you today?

Quack, quack, quack, come out to play!

Puppy, how are you today?

Bark, bark, bark, come out to play!

Owlet, in the bright moonlight,

Hooo, hooo, time to say good night!

Adventure
Learning Press

adventurelearningpress.com